Snakes

WELDON OWEN PTY LTD

Chairman: John Owen
Publisher: Sheena Coupe
Associate Publisher: Lynn Humphries
Managing Editor: Helen Bateman
Design Concept: Sue Rawkins
Senior Designer: Kylie Mulquin
Production Manager: Caroline Webber
Production Assistant: Kylie Lawson

Text: Sharon Dalgleish
Consultant: George McKay, Conservation Biologist
U.S. Editors: Laura Cavaluzzo and Rebecca McEwen

© 1999 Weldon Owen Inc.

04 03 02 01 00
10 9 8 7 6 5 4 3 2

Published in the United States by
Shortland Publications, Inc.
P.O. Box 6195
Denver, CO 80206-0195

Printed in Singapore.
ISBN: 0-7699-0479-3

CONTENTS

Sizing Up Snakes

There are almost 2,400 different species of snakes in the world. They come in all sizes, colors, and patterns. The vine snake of South America grows to 7 feet (2 meters), but its slim body is no more than ½ inch (1.3 centimeters) thick. Your finger is probably thicker! The giant anaconda can weigh up to 440 pounds (200 kilograms)—about as heavy as you and six friends.

Built-in Oar
A sea snake has a flattened tail, which gives the snake an extra push through the water.

DID YOU KNOW?

The rat snake got its name
because it likes to eat mice
and rats. The rat snake uses dry
leaves to trick and scare away
predators. It vibrates its tail
among the leaves, making a
sound like a rattlesnake.

Perfect Camouflage
The green color of the vine snake
helps it to blend in with leaves.
Its slender body helps it to
move quickly across branches.

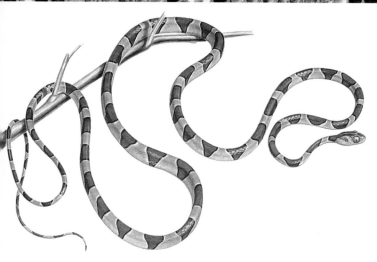

Between the Branches
The blunt-headed tree snake of Central and South America has a long, flattened body.

Snakes have different body shapes to suit the different environments in which they live. A tree snake has a flattened body that can grip small notches on branches. A viper's short, thick body is well camouflaged so it can hide to ambush its prey. A python has a large, circular body with strong muscles. Some of the largest snakes are pythons.

Hidden Danger
The rhinoceros viper's pattern helps it hide in fallen leaves.

Swamp Lover

The blood python lives in the swamps and rainforest streams of Southeast Asia.

Day and Night

Snakes that are active in daylight have large eyes that they use to see their prey. Snakes that are active at night have small eyes. They don't need sight to find their prey. Instead, they use their tongues or special heat-sensing organs.

big eyes

small eyes

7

On Their Own
Baby snakes have to
face many predators,
including other snakes.

EARLY LIFE

Most snakes simply lay their eggs and then leave
their young to develop and hatch on their own.
Some snakes, such as water snakes, give birth to live
young. Snakes may change the way they look as they
grow older. Newly hatched green tree pythons are
bright yellow or brown. It can take up to three years
for a baby tree python to turn into a green adult.

DID YOU KNOW?

Some pythons behave differently from other snakes—they coil around their eggs to protect them from predators. Sometimes they shiver to make heat to keep the eggs warm.

lungs, also became long and thin. Others were rearranged one behind the other in the body. In many snakes the left lung disappeared. In others, the second lung is very small and does not work.

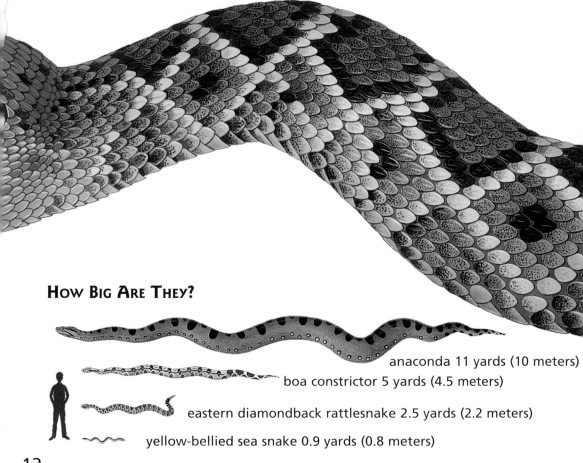

How Big Are They?

anaconda 11 yards (10 meters)

boa constrictor 5 yards (4.5 meters)

eastern diamondback rattlesnake 2.5 yards (2.2 meters)

yellow-bellied sea snake 0.9 yards (0.8 meters)

INSIDE A SNAKE

Snakes are reptiles, like lizards. They are long and thin so they can squeeze into narrow spaces to escape predators or chase prey. As snakes evolved, some of their organs, such as the liver and the

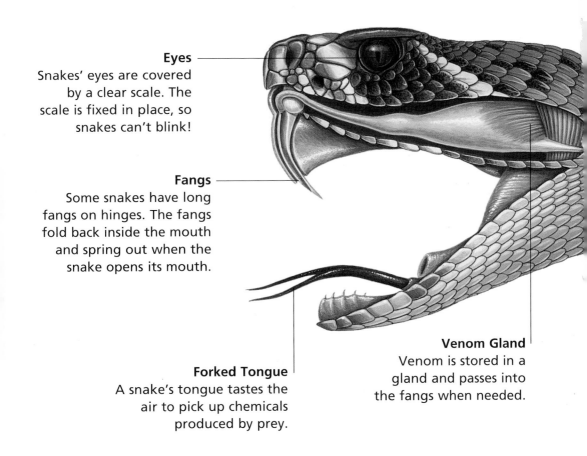

Eyes
Snakes' eyes are covered by a clear scale. The scale is fixed in place, so snakes can't blink!

Fangs
Some snakes have long fangs on hinges. The fangs fold back inside the mouth and spring out when the snake opens its mouth.

Forked Tongue
A snake's tongue tastes the air to pick up chemicals produced by prey.

Venom Gland
Venom is stored in a gland and passes into the fangs when needed.

New and Old Scales

A rattlesnake has a number of thickened scaly sections in its tail. These produce its famous rattle. Every time it sheds its skin, it gains a new section. The oldest segment is always at the tip of the tail.

Scaly Skin

Snakes have scaly skin to protect them from rough ground as they slither along. Even their eyes are protected by clear scales instead of eyelids. When a snake grows too big for its skin, it sheds it— there's always a new skin growing underneath. To loosen its skin, a snake rubs its nose against something hard like a rock. The old skin, including the clear eyelids, peels off inside out. Then the snake wriggles free.

Useful Scales
Snake scales can be rough or smooth, depending on where the snake lives. Some even have a keel like a boat.

rough   keel   smooth

...o stay
...has less
...eep heat

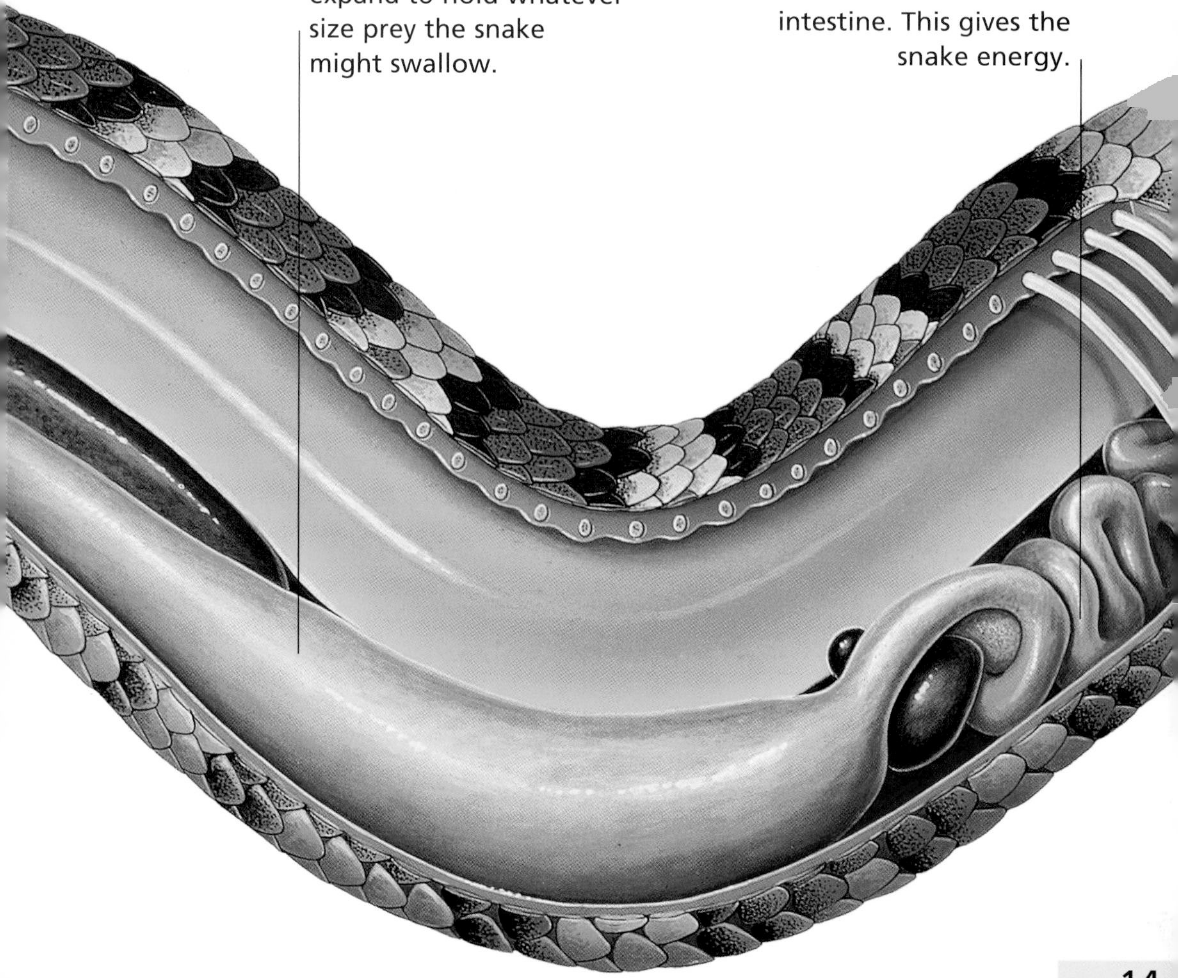

Stomach
A snake's stomach can expand to hold whatever size prey the snake might swallow.

Small Intestine
Food is absorbed into the bloodstream from the small intestine. This gives the snake energy.

A snake can change its body shape t
warm or cool. A tightly coiled snake
surface area exposed, which helps k
from being lost or gained.

Lungs
Most snakes have one
narrow lung that can
run nearly the length
of their body.

Ribs
A snake's backbone can
have between 150 and
450 vertebrae. Each
vertebra has two ribs.

Liver
The liver filters and
cleans the blood. A snake
has a very long liver.

13

ON THE MOVE

To move without legs, snakes lever themselves on their belly scales and push with muscles attached to the ribs. They use their body in different ways to move on different surfaces. A few desert snakes move across loose sand sideways. The snake anchors its head and tail in the sand, and lifts a loop of its body clear of the hot ground. This is called sidewinding.

Slow and Heavy
Many heavy snakes crawl by pushing back with sections of their belly while bringing other sections forward.

DID YOU KNOW?

The flying tree snake can glide through the air to escape predators in trees. It launches itself into the air with its belly curved in, which acts like a parachute.

Rear Fangs

Rear fangs have grooves that the venom travels along.

Fixed Front Fangs

Cobras have hollow fangs fixed in the front of the mouth.

Swinging Front Fangs

Vipers and rattlesnakes have hollow fangs that swing forward to strike.

VENOMOUS SNAKES

Some snakes can paralyze or kill their prey with poison called venom. Snake venom is so powerful that it can work within minutes, sometimes even seconds! One venom works on the nerves to stop the heart and paralyze the lungs. Another works by destroying muscles. The venom comes from glands in the snake's head, through fangs, and into its mouth. Snakes with hollow fangs inject venom into their prey. Snakes with grooved rear fangs must chew their prey for the venom to ooze in.

OPEN WIDE

A snake can move its bones apart and stretch its mouth to swallow large prey. It has elastic connections between the bones in its bottom jaw. A snake usually swallows prey head first so the animal's legs don't stick in its throat. A big python can swallow a wild pig! Such a big meal can take weeks—or even months—to digest.

Feet First
Frogs puff themselves up with air so they're hard to swallow, but snakes just swallow them feet first and push the air out.

A stomach bulging with dinner slows a snake down and makes it hard to escape danger. Snakes with a full stomach often lie in a sunny, sheltered spot. The heat helps speed up digestion.

FINDING FOOD

Stabbing Fangs
Some snakes have fangs to stab venom into their prey.

Snakes eat a variety of animal life, including insects, frogs, rats, and other snakes. More than half of all snakes kill their prey with venom injected through fangs. Pythons and boa constrictors squeeze their prey to death. They wrap themselves around their prey, squeezing a little tighter every time the animal breathes out, until it suffocates.

King of the Snakes
The king snake hunts and eats other snakes—even venomous rattlesnakes! Strangely, rattlesnakes don't bite back when they are attacked by a king snake.

The night snake has large teeth at the rear of its mouth, but they are not true fangs. The snake grabs a lizard quickly and pulls it to the back of its mouth. Poisonous saliva slowly kills the lizard.

Shiny Strangler
The Brazilian rainbow boa suffocates its prey.

Night Ambush

The urutu uses scent to find pathways used by its prey. It coils itself and waits, ready for ambush.

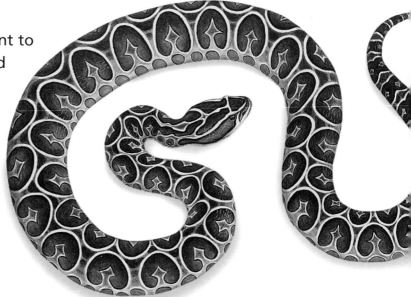

Sudden Death

The Mojave rattlesnake hunts small mammals. It is easily excited and is one of the most dangerous snakes in the United States.

Some snakes eat eggs and other prey that are easy to find. Other snakes are active hunters. They use heat sensors to tell how far away they are from their prey, and even to target an animal's heart. Some snakes like to ambush their prey. They will wait for days, often camouflaged, for suitable prey to come along.

Tasty Snacks
The banded sand snake burrows in the desert sand to eat ant eggs.

AMAZING!

The cottonmouth is a type of pit viper. It has such a strong reflex action that even when its head has been chopped off, the head will sometimes still bite!

25

Clever Camouflage
The brown vine snake's shape and color match its surroundings.

DEFENSE TACTICS

Snakes have many enemies. They can be killed and eaten by fish, lizards, other snakes, birds, and mammals. Many snakes have clever ways of defending themselves. The hog-nosed snake pretends to be dead to confuse predators. Even if it's touched, it doesn't move. If the predator still won't go away, the snake releases a terrible smell! Other snakes bury themselves to hide from danger.

False Colors

The false coral snake looks just like the venomous coral snake! The only difference is the red in the harmless snake's tail.

Puff Adder

A puff adder is normally hard to see because its color helps it blend into the background. If it is threatened, it puffs up its body and hisses loudly as it tries to back away.

Warning Sounds

The rattlesnake rattles its tail to warn large animals not to step on it.

A Frightening Sight
The harmless vine snake startles predators by opening wide its brightly colored mouth.

Many harmless snakes have bright colors and patterns that are similar to those of venomous snakes. The bright colors spell danger and warn predators to keep away. Some snakes wave their tail to draw attention away from their head. The waving tail looks like a head about to strike. Others surprise their enemies by hissing or by lashing out. Some escape by slithering quickly up a tree.

Warning Signal

The Pacific gopher snake will strike to defend itself—but first it gives a warning signal. It hisses loudly and vibrates its tail tip when it is angry.

Look-alike

The Louisiana milk snake looks like the venomous coral snake. This protects it from predators.

GLOSSARY

camouflage Something in an animal's appearance that allows it to blend into its surroundings, so it can stay safe, or catch food.

digestion The process that breaks down food inside the body of an animal.

fangs Long, sharp teeth that spiders and snakes use to inject poison into their prey.

heat-sensing organs Special organs that some snakes have, which detect tiny changes in temperature.

jaw One of the upper or lower bones that form the mouth and hold any teeth the animal might have.

keel The ridge running along the bottom of a boat that helps keep the boat balanced in the water. Snakes' scales often form a ridge like a boat's keel.

predators Animals that hunt and kill other animals.

prey Animals that are caught and eaten by other animals.

venom Poison that is injected by certain animals to attack enemies, or by plants to trap food.

vertebrae The bones that form an animal's spine.

INDEX

CREDITS AND NOTES

Picture and Illustration Credits
[t=top, b=bottom, l=left, r=right, c=center, F=front, B=back, C=cover, bg=background]
Anne Bowman 21tr. **Corel Corporation** 10tr, 13tl, 22tl, 23tc, 24bl, 25cr, 25bl, 26tr, 29c, 29bc. **Simone End** 7br, 10/15c, 28tr, FCc, FCrc. **Christer Eriksson** 3tr, 18tr, 20–21c. **John Francis/Bernard Thornton Artists UK** 18–19bc, 18tl, 18lc, 18bl. **David Kirshner** 1c, 4bc, 5c, 6tl, 6–7bc, 7tl, 11–14c, 12bl, 15b, 20lc, 22bc, 23c, 24tc, 27cl, 27br, 28cl, 30tr, BC, FCtl. **Frank Knight** 2b, 8–9c, 8tl, 9br, 30bl. **PhotoDisc** 4–32 borders, Cbg. **Oliver Rennert** 27rc. **Trevor Ruth** 4–5c, 16t, 16b, 16–17c, 17br.

Acknowledgements
Weldon Owen would like to thank the following people for their assistance in the production of this book:
Jocelyne Best, Peta Gorman, Tracey Jackson, Andrew Kelly, Sarah Mattern, Emily Wood.